WARDROBE ESSENTIALS

The Top Ten Clothing and Accessory Choices for a Workable Wardrobe

By Judith Rasband

To order additional copies of this book, contact:
Xlibris
844-714-8691
www.Xlibris.com
Orders@Xlibris.com

ISBN: 978-1-6641-5707-1 (sc)
ISBN: 978-1-6641-5706-4 (e)

Print information available on the last page

Rev. date: 02/19/2021

Introduction

Read My Words

People allow themselves to think of clothing as trivial, assuming clothing to be superfluous. Some pretend, "Clothes don't matter." Others argue, "Attention to clothing is vain." Nonsense! I ask you, "When was the last time you went out without your clothes on?" A naked woman, has no influence.

I say that clothing fills a basic need for survival in the world and communication to the world. Like shelter and food, clothing is a basic resource we need to learn how to use for our benefit. Clothing has universal effects, affecting the way we think, the way we feel, the way we act or behave, and only then the way others react or respond to us. We need to learn how to control these effects for our benefit.

This book is written for *you*. With this book I want to make you more aware of the everyday aspects of dress and dressing. I want to enable you to use your clothing as a resource, a tool to help you think, feel, and act better throughout your day—your closet being your toolbox.

You'll read about *image from the outside in*—the effects or influence of your clothing on you, and about *image from the inside out*—the effects or influence of your clothing on others and the achievement of your goals. This is a book about *you*, about bringing your outer self into harmony or in sync with your inner self.

I will identify specific pieces of clothing and accessories proven to work effectively to simplify your life, with additional options allowing more creativity and individuality if you want it. I'll touch on the language of clothing as a form of non-verbal communication. There is actual meaning attached to what you wear and how you wear it. I want you to begin to see, to recognize the characteristics, traits, cues or clues that you can use to express yourself and aid you in the achievement of your life goals.

"The eye can see only what the mind has been prepared to comprehend."

—Robertson Davies
Playwright

WARDROBE ESSENTIALS

The Top Ten Clothing and Accessory Choices for a Stylish Wardrobe That Works

You've had your breakfast, showered, groomed yourself as best you can be, but now you have only 10 minutes to dress before you head out for the day. You open your closet door and think, "So what'll I wear?" Or, you mutter the age old cliché, "I have nothing to wear." Well, you may have plenty to wear, but nothing you really want to wear. That's the real problem and many people can relate.

Maybe you overslept, the kids needed help, or a friend called early to tell you some great news. It happens. Whatever, you're running late and you don't know what to wear so you grab the same old standbys just to get you out the door. Yes, you may be able to forget about yourself and get on with your day, but chances are you're hung up to some degree—not looking, not feeling, not acting your best all day long. Students and clients not feeling comfortable with themselves, tell me they do hang back a little and seldom go out of their way for anything or anybody. Not a good way to go.

Yes, there's a better way to go. Decide what to wear the night before. I call it my "Tomorrow" exercise, wherein you learn to ask yourself:

- Where will I be going tomorrow?
- What will I be doing?
- Who will be with me, will see me?
- What do I need or want to accomplish?
- What statement or message do I want my clothes to communicate?
- What clothes will communicate that message? And do I know why?

OK, but how do you get a closet stocked with all the right clothes? What makes up the perfect wardrobe? A classic cluster? Essential pieces of clothing that will allow you to avoid the kind of morning described above?

You have to take action! You start with a plan—a plan with a purpose. Plan to invest your time, effort, and money in smart clothing choices that keep you feeling confident—ready to meet any challenge the day brings—and credible as a woman who plans to lead and inspire family, colleagues, or clients for years to come.

That means buying into the topic. It's the details of discussion about them that differ—some great, some good, bad, or downright ridiculous. It seems that each new generation has to discover them all over again. As a matter of fact, they often think they invented them. Not so. The reason these pieces persist time and again is obvious. They work!

Some women want to avoid daily concern with dress. They'll even admit they want a uniform so they don't have to think about what to wear. The following pieces actually fit that need—with a little more variety. With basic, classic pieces like these in a wardrobe neutral color and all-season fabric, you will worry less about what to wear, experience more confidence and actual joy when dressing for your day, and life will become easier. How's that for a plan with benefits?! The pieces include:

Top Ten Clothing Essentials List	Top Ten Accessory Essentials List
1. Blazer Jacket	1. Flat Shoes
2. Pencil Straight Skirt	2. High Heels
3. Straight Leg Slacks	3. Brief Bag
4. Little Basic Dress	4. Clutch Bag
5. Cardigan Sweater	5. Belt
6. Vest	6. Jewelry
7. Button-Front Shirt	7. Glasses
8. Pullover Shirt	8. Scarf
9. Dress Jeans	9. Hat
10. Trench Coat	10. Stockings

For some women, no further reading is necessary. They get it without further explanation or discussion. They go and buy these essential pieces and wear them regularly. They know intuitively to gradually find and buy—to add on—three to four or more tops to wear with their skirt and pants. Gradually they'll expand their wardrobe to include a new cluster of clothes, knowing that many of the new pieces will work well with their wardrobe essentials. For specific occasions when they feel the need to present themselves classically and with some degree of visual authority, they wear their wardrobe essentials. Most women benefit by reading about each wardrobe essential piece.

Top Ten Clothing Essentials

You can read a little or read some more. Review often.

Blazer Jacket

A single-breasted blazer is an essential piece in any wardrobe whether you're 15 or 55. If you think you're "not a jacket person," let me tease by saying, "Get over it." A classic blazer is an essential third layer garment that looks amazing worn over a shirt, sweater, or vest, skirt, slacks, or jeans. You have the option of wearing your blazer over your basic day dress as well as over a simple evening dress. To learn to like wearing a jacket, you just have to get some experience wearing one. It'll win you over. Who knows, you may even become a real "jacket person."

Semi-fitted Blazer

Fitted Blazer

Select a basic blazer made of a fabulous light- to medium-weight fabric, relatively smooth, without adornment or flashy decoration. That's what allows the blazer to transition from day to evening and from season to season, depending on what you choose to wear it with. Designed with a collar and lapel, that's what lifts attention upward to your face for better communication. Choose a one, two, or threebutton style—the longer the lapel the more visual authority it conveys. Wear your blazer open or closed, with sophisticated style, comfort, and ease. Rely on your blazer as a quick way to upgrade a casual looking outfit. It's what transforms your basic shirt and skirt or jeans and tee into a powerful positive impression, in or out of the office.

Princess-seam Blazer

Nothing pulls together your basics and completes a slim looking outfit better than a blazer. Select a fitted blazer or fuller straight cut style, depending on your body build. You're smart to select a crotchlength blazer. Yes, everybody can wear a crotch-length blazer. Men's suit jackets, sport jackets, and blazers are generally cut and hemmed at crotch length and no one tells a shorter man he can't wear them or that they "cut him in half" as is regularly said to shorter women. Truth be known, wear your blazer open over a contrasting colored shirt and you create a vertical line that draws attention inward for a dress-slim effect and vertically up and down for a lengthening effect. At crotch length, a blazer also camouflages a larger midriff, tummy, side thighs, and behind. Why do you think men's jackets hang to there? They work!

More about blazers…..

Wrap Blazer

Unfitted Blazer

Whether your waist is high or low it makes little difference in a blazer because the waist area is less defined. If you want to show off a shapely waistline, select a fitted blazer or have it altered in the side seamlines to fit you—very effective. A blazer jacket should hang smoothly from your shoulders and fit with enough ease to comfortably accommodate a shirt and sweater or vest underneath. Shoulder seams should set on the end of your shoulder bones. The hem of long sleeves must fit right at your wrists, not half-way down your hand looking like you borrowed daddy's jacket. If you are five-foot-four or shorter, look for petite sizing scaled down in the proportional length to better fit you.

Most blazers are made with set-in shoulder pads. Yes I know, most women think they hate shoulder pads, don't want shoulder pads when they're not "in fashion." I'm not talking about huge, broad, thick football pads. I'm talking "moderate" in size and shape. Truth be known, shoulder pads fill out your shoulders, allowing the jacket to angle inward toward the waist creating the illusion of a slightly narrower waist for a dress-slimmer look. They also serve to balance wider hips and thighs. Forever more, think of shoulder pads as fitting tools, not fashion trends. They work wonders!

Blazers are terrific! You have so many varieties of fabric to choose from as add-ons, including fabrics in denim, corduroy, leather or lowcost "pleather." They let you play up your personal style layered over a dress, sportshirt, graphic tee, skirt, pants, or colored jeans. You can finish your outfit with a fun or classy lapel pin, a lacy or patterned pocket square, a silky or textured scarf. My own favorite black blazer for years was an absolutely divine polyester microfiber, with longer lapels—all the more able to slim and lift my look with a little visual authority. I rolled up the sleeves to three-quarter length to further slim and relax my look, countering with a right-angle gold lapel pin that drew attention upward near my face for quality communication. We have options.

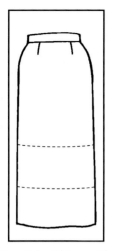

Straight Skirt with
length options

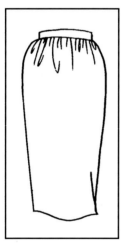

Tapered Skirt with
added fulllness

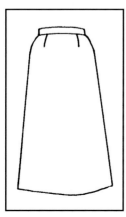

A-line Skirt

Pencil Straight Skirt

This is the simplest basic skirt there is and so sophisticated. Ideally made of the same fabric as your jacket, it mixes with all of your basic, classic essentials. You can easily dress it up or dress it down for day or evening, summer or winter. Waist-fitting is classic. Even then, don't over-fit a straight skirt. You should be able to "pinch-n-inch" of ease on each side at hip level. When so tight that the skirt "cups under" your bottom, it's too tight. Tight horizontal wrinkles form around your hips in front and diagonal drag lines point exactly to your bottom in back! That's too much information and attention on your backside. Classic skirt hemlines are center of the knee, or two inches below the knee—exactly at the natural indentation just below the knee and above the calf. Fashion hemlines are one inch or more above the knee, and just below the calf. Mid-calf length tends to enlarge the look of the leg—generally not flattering.

A pencil straight skirt doesn't always fit or flatter every body. If you live in a triangular or an hour-glass figure type, it nearly never fits because you're smaller in the waist and bigger in the bottom. If the straight skirt fits your smaller waist, it's always too small in the bottom or the hip-thigh area. If it fits your bigger bottom and hip-thigh area, it's always too big in the waist. That's typical of these figure types. If you live in an inverted triangle or diamond figure type, it's just the reverse. You're larger in the waist and smaller in the bottom. If you live in a rectangular figure type, you're larger in the waist. Sometimes the skirt fits because waistlines are being made larger these days.

Sometimes it doesn't. A straight skirt may not even fit an ideal figure because every designer/manufacturer works with a different set of measurements. To simplify the fit, try on straight skirts with a little stretch in the fabric, from 2 to 5% Lycra, so they're less apt to wrinkle during the day and don't become baggy with wear. Nonetheless, a pencil straight skirt often has to be altered by a tailor to fit your body well.

More about skirts…..

To avoid fitting and alteration problems altogether, choose a flared skirt instead of straight. A flared skirt is the easiest and most flattering skirt style for most women to wear. A-line works if you're slim, but seldom fits over the larger hip-thigh area of the triangular figure type. Even then, if cut on the straight grain, the sides stick out, looking more like wings. Cut on the diagonal bias, the fit is more flattering because the minimal flare is distributed all around the figure. Which brings me back to flared skirts as the most flattering for all figures because there is more flare to begin with. To

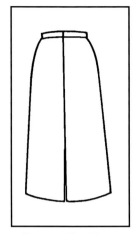

Center Slit Skirt

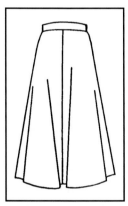

4-Gore Flared Skirt

avoid looking bulky, the more flare in the skirt, the lighter-weight the fabric must be.

Now, if you really want or need an easy fit, select a skirt with elastic in the waistband—better yet, in the back waistline only. No, elastic does not always add bulk. Generally, higher quality skirts feature narrower, flat-lying elastic. If it looks bulky, don't buy it. No, elastic does not need to look "old lady," as many say so disrespectfully. Look for elastic used in the back only, and even then you can cover it with a fantastic belt or layer with a top, sweater, vest, or jacket. Generally avoid mid-calf length skirts because they are hemmed exactly at the widest part of the calf, creating the illusion of added width. Long maxi-skirts are generally more flattering, versatile, and comfortable to wear than short mini-skirts.

For variety, additional skirts added over the years might include a pleated skirt, gathered dirndl skirt, a tiered skirt, an asymmetrical hem or an angular handkerchief hem skirt, maybe a curved high-low skirt. Take yourself snoop-shopping once in awhile and try on a few to find out which ones feel like *you*.

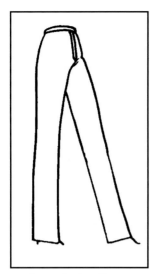

Straight-leg Pants

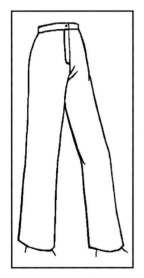

Stovepipe Pants

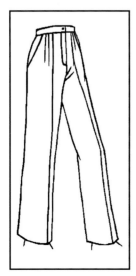

Pleat-front Trousers

Straight Leg Slacks

Call them pants, slacks, or trousers—the difference is in the degree of refinement in the fabric and the quality of construction. Straight leg style or stovepipe, the simplest basic, classic yet sophisticated pant there is, taking you places in style where a dress or skirt just won't do. Ideally made of the same marvelous material as your jacket, it works well with all of your wardrobe essentials. These pants are made for multitasking when you change roles during the day—they take you virtually anywhere you need to go. You can easily dress them down or dress them up for day or evening, in summer or winter weather. Without a pair your wardrobe is essentially non-functional!

Fitting expert par none, I know what it takes for a *Fabulous Fit,* and pants fitting is the most difficult. Basic, classic pants need to fit at your natural waistline—no low riders to confuse your waistline with the distracting muffin top they impose below your waist. You need a smooth fit in the waist, cut close to your crotch in front. These pants are designed to fit smoothly over your front thighs, no bulging or pulling over the inside, front, or outside of your thigh. Unlike the pencil straight skirt, straight-leg pants are often designed cup under just a little below your bottom, still with some ease. Stuck in your crotch is too much information—crude and rude. It's common for ready-towear pants to fit in the waist but not in the hip-thigh area, or fit in the hip-thigh area but not in the waist. Don't hesitate to buy for the hipthigh area and have the waist altered to fit. I have to do it for myself and clients all the time. Straight-leg pants are hemmed with one fold (or break) at the top of your instep so you can wear them with flats or heels. If you want custom-fit pants, call me.

More about straight leg slacks…..

Should you choose flat-front pants or pants designed with trouser pleats? The inexperienced fashionista will advise "slimming, flat-front pants," claiming that "trouser pleats only accentuate an area that no one really needs accentuating." Bad advice. Flat-front pants are not slimming on all. They are designed with waist-fitting darts shaped so they actually define a tummy bulge. Trouser pleat pants made with flatlying fabric can actually be the most flattering on most figures. They're terrific when you want a more tailored look. Made of lighter-weight fabric, flat-lying trouser pleats can flow smoothly over a tummy so as not to cup back under and expose the tummy bulge.

Leggings are not to be confused with slacks or pants of any sort. Pants they are not. If added on to your wardrobe after you have acquired your basic, classic straight leg slacks, leggings are to be worn with a top that covers your bottom. Your options include a tunic length shirt, sweater, vest, or jacket, a dress or a duster—all readily available in retail stores, catalogs, and online. A lady and a leader does not go public with her bottom exposed to view, rippling provocatively as she walks. Too much information! If you want to be taken seriously, cover your bottom!

Little Basic Dress

Fashion mavens have recently lost sight of what the "little black dress" was originally designed to be. Coco Chanel introduced this simple dress to the world in 1926. The LBD, be it a little black dress or a little basic dress, "black" and "basic" define the garment Coco designed to go with virtually everything and take you virtually everywhere in style and grace. Having one in your closet can prevent a total meltdown every time you get a last-minute invitation to a special event.

Universal and individual at the same time, simple sheath, shift, A-line, side-wrap, and shirtwaist styles with a moderate scoop or V-neckline and three-quarter or long sleeves lend themselves to layering with a variety of vests, sweaters, jackets, jewelry, scarves, and belts.

Shoes for this dress can range from ballet flats to heels, and boots. Worn with pearls or a pendant, you get to develop your own personal style. Think of it as your multitasking dress made appropriate for a luncheon or leadership, in church or the office, shopping or symphony. Invest in the best quality all-season fabric and construction you can afford. It will pay off in the low cost-per-wearing. Light to medium weight crepe fabric is an excellent option.

The little black dress is actually not so little. It's got to fit your whole body perfectly. Ideally the LBD should be lined or worn with a slip so the fabric skims easily over your figure. Classic and attractive sleeve lengths are two inches above the elbow, three-quarter length just below the elbow, and full length to the wrist. If arms are smooth and firm, cap sleeves and sleeveless styles become additional options. Classic skirt lengths are middle-of-the-knee and just above or just below the knee, with a dressy fashion length at just below the calf.

More about a dress.....

Once you've got your classic LBD, you can add on other dresses, be they for day or evening. Your choice of fabric tells the story. It might be made out of denim or gingham, crinkle cloth or knit for day. We so often wear pants, but a shift or an A-line dress is actually a more comfortable and surprising change of pace. For evening, a dress looks dressier when made out of softly draped fabric, shiny or metallic fabric, or fancy fabric embellished with beads and sequins. The skirt is often wrapped, flared and floaty, or full. This dress may seem less practical but you feel fabulous whenever it comes out of the closet, time and time again, taking you to special occasions in your life—and that's worth every penny.

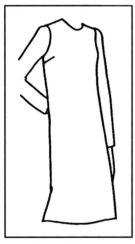

Sheath Dress

Shift Dress

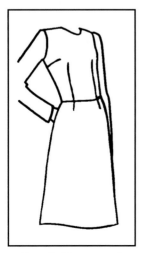

Sheath Dress with
Waist Seam

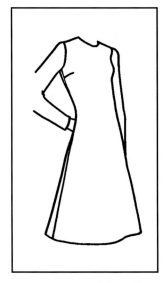

A-line Dress

Flared Dress

Cardigan Sweater

Sweater Set

Cardigan Sweater

Another great layering piece is a classic long-sleeved cardigan sweater. It can take the place of a jacket, just softer in look, feel, and effect. Worn layered for some visual authority, it works in the home, out in the community, as well as in a more relaxed office—especially in summer if you're stuck in a ridiculously cold air-conditioned location. Never bulky, it even works worn over summer tops or a sundress as the evening turns chilly.

For durability, choose a medium weight, tightly knitted cardigan. I've worn the same classic black cardigan for decades and it still looks, feels, and fits terrific. Choices include wool for winter, durable cotton for summer, cotton if you're allergic to wool. Merino wool is wonderful in winter, but too heavy and hot for many women. Cashmere is luxuriously soft year 'round, but balls up or "pills" easily (fibers break away from the thread or yarn and forms little balls of fiber, called pilling). High quality wool is more refined so slightly dressier, isn't scratchy, has less pilling, holds its shape, and retains its color. Acrylic imitates wool but also pills. Wash gently and make time to remove the pills.

Your cardigan should fit with enough ease—it doesn't pull around your chest, midriff, upper back, lower back, or belly. It glides smoothly over your body without clinging or adding bulk. Yes, choose a crotchlength cardigan for smoother body lines. No, not in any bright color your heart desires. Again, something bright is going to be an add-on after you have your basic. Black is basic—or whatever wardrobe neutral you choose to work with.

Worn open with a pencil skirt and shirt, the look is more approachable for a planning meeting or out to a movie. Worn over a t-shirt and jeans, the look is perfect for a jaunt to the store or the kids ball game. A cardigan is great for those times when you don't know what the weather's going to be where you're going. Drape or tie a cardigan around your shoulders over a dress, shirt, or pullover sweater—it doubles as a collar, lifting the look and framing your face.

More about cardigan sweaters…..

Yes, a twinset is an option, the pullover piece could take the place of your essential knit top. Problem is, you end up wearing it alone with your skirt, pants, and jeans, wearing it out before the cardigan is ready to give up the ghost. I'd save a great twinset as an add-on, after you have your basic essential cardigan.

Be it a heavier wool knit for winter, a lightweight cashmere, or a multi-colored open knit polyester for summer, there's a plain or patterned cardigan "out there" for every body. Solid color first, then add patterned, possibly in stripes or a new print floral. When concerned about a change in the temperature, you can stash a cardigan in your classy tote bag more easily than a jacket, or tie it around the strap of your bag.

Fitted Vest

Low-Hip Vest

Unfitted Vest

Button-Front Vest

The most forgotten piece of clothing on my list is a vest. A vest, also called a waistcoat, is a sleeveless third-layer garment perfect to wear year 'round without the weight and warmth of a jacket. A vest fills out and adds visual authority to an outfit, yet flows over your figure to camouflage extra pounds for a flattering fit. Add to that, when worn open, a vest forms that slimming vertical line at center-front. Armholes are often larger and/or longer than in a shirt, making it super easy and comfortable to fit—leaving your arms free for action.

Many vests are designed with a collar, which upgrades the look of a collarless dress or top—a particularly great way to power up the look of a t-shirt. Like a blazer, vests come short and long. Choose the length that works best for your body—longer if you have a full-rounded abdomen, bottom, or side-thighs. Your essential vest needs to be woven fabric, smooth, and sleek, able to layer harmoniously over the other fabrics in your wardrobe essentials. Hm-m-m, you might also find a lightweight smooth leather or suede vest. Options are out there. Vests with button, snap, zipper, or drawstring closures can be relatively basic and classic. Sometimes a vest may feature a fold of fabric at center front, a bit like a lapel—no fasteners at all.

More about vests.....

When you're ready to think about add-ons to your wardrobe think about adding an interesting vest. Styles include fitted Victorian vests, loose-fitting fisherman vests, military vests, safari vests, hooded vests, sweater vests, longline duster vests, and maxi-length vests—single and double-breasted varieties, with a band, funnel, or cascade collar, and diagonal zipper or toggle fasteners. The variety of fabrics and weights available add to the fun in selection, ranging from sheer gauze, voile, or crocheted vests to denim, textured leather, suede, shearling, boiled wool, faux fur, and quilted puffer vests.

Sport Shirt
Button Placket

Shoulder Yoke Shirt
Hidden Buttons

Sport Shirt Shirt-tail Hem

Button-Front Shirt

A classy white shirt is generally considered essential for every woman's wardrobe, but don't panic if it's not your style. I'll give you other options. I recommend a woven medium-weight fabric, cotton broadcloth dress shirt with medium scale collar and cuffs—nothing stiff. A collar lifts attention and frames your face for better communication. The look of a crisp white shirt is sophisticated, even with jeans. A white shirt elevates the look of a pencil skirt or slacks and finishes the look of a tailored business suit. Nonetheless, it can look more relaxed when belted on the outside or layered underneath a v-neck sweater or a vest. Roll up the long sleeves to further relax to look if you like.

Yes, it looks much like a man's white dress shirt, also available in a tapered cut for a closer slim fit or straight cut for a fuller fit. If there is any pulling or gaping at the bust or midriff, buy a larger size! If size won't fix the fitting problem, select a larger style shirt with a shoulder yoke controlling darts, gathers, or pleats above the bust. If you want more shape to your shirt, you can add lengthwise waist-fitting darts— or go to an alterations shop where a tailor can do it for you. Slightly fitted styles, rather than straight-cut, are easier to tuck into a skirt or pants and look neater when belted or worn loose.

Make sure you get a "no-iron" fabric guaranteed to retain its crisp looking press for up to 25 to 30 washings. When that's an option, neck sweater or a vest. Roll up the long sleeves to further relax the look if you like. many of us must admit we really don't take time to iron very often. Upgrade your white shirt with French cuffs if you like. Omit any trim or decorative detail on this basic wardrobe item. With time, you may end up with more than one white shirt. But always, buy only the shirts that lie smooth around the collar. Add a favorite textured scarf, necklace, bracelet, or belt to finish an outfit according to your personal style.

More about woven button-front shirts.....

Some have said or written that you can't wear white? Nonsense! They just don't know how to do it attractively. Feel free to wear a white shirt whenever you want to look crisp, fresh, and full of life, even in winter. Simply add more contrast to your look with a little blush and mascara, a jacket, or a medium to darker color scarf containing the color of your hair, eyes, or blush—or all three. Do not limit your options but color yourself smart!

Unfitted Shirt
Square-cut Hem

Safari Shirt

Camp Shirt

Some have written that you always have to wear your shirt tucked in. Again, nonsense. It's an option, depending on your figure type and what you want to communicate. Extremely triangular figure types do not want to tuck in their shirt unless they layer the look to fill out their shoulders and create a smooth transitional line from shoulder to below the hip. Wearing your shirt tucked into a skirt or pants looks and says "orderly, organized, sharp." Loosen the shirt so it "blouses" about one inch outward at the waist, making hips and thighs appear narrower below. Belt if you like, reinforcing the orderly appearance. Wearing your shirt un-tucked looks and says "relaxed, sporty." Partially tucked in front says that following a trend is important to you, whether it works or not.

Sleeveless shirts work only for women with firm arms. Soft body "Jello" arms are unattractive at any age. Make sure armholes are high enough so your bra is not exposed and distracting. A sleeveless shirt is an option for all women when worn under a blazer or cardigan, still looking crisp but cooler. Let me say it now, if a white shirt isn't part of your personal style— you prefer something more feminine or elegant—opt for a silk shirt in ivory or a rich jewel tone such as sapphire blue, ruby red, emerald green, amethyst, purple, or topaz. Both color and fabric are luxurious, in harmony with a high level professional or leadership look.

If you lead a more relaxed lifestyle, choose instead, a blue chambray sport shirt. The look is less refined and more relaxed— terrific to dress down black slacks or complement your jeans. It hints at the possibility of a little more fun in the making. Top it with your blazer or cardigan sweater. Wear it open as a shirt-jac over a tank, tee, or turtleneck, depending on the weather. You've got options.

Yes, I know that many women are going to tell me they sweat a lot and will ruin a white or a silk shirt. I understand you don't want to spend your money on those. So let's figure out how to do it so you're not left with a bunch of lower quality tops. First of all, they don't always have to be expensive. Mindfully, plan to shop the sales, knowing already where to find higher quality shirts at the price you can afford. Make a lightweight shell part of your underwear, intended to protect the white or silk fabric. Underarm shields are another option and prescription-strength antiperspirants are available. Add to that, greatgrandma was right. If possible, hang your shirt outside a couple of days to freshen it so you can get two or three wearings in before washing or cleaning.

V-Neck Shell

Scoop-neck Shell

Pullover Shirt

White is generally the essential color for this basic, classic top, generally a knit. Knit necklines easily lose their shape and stain easily. Buy into several better quality ones when on sale and replace any you're wearing the day it starts to look worn out. Medium-weight cotton knit is generally the fabric, or possibly a blend. It must be opaque and not a flimsy thin-knit. I recommend a scoop or V-neckline, not an "underwear" t-shirt with a round crew neckline. Both scoop and V-necklines are more flattering. Designed with straight lines and an angle, V-neckline packs more power or visual authority, communicating more capability on your part. Make it a moderate V-shape, exposing no cleavage to counter your credibility. A scoop neckline looks more approachable and allows for more options in necklaces. The basic scoop should lie near or on your breastbone. Choose a pullover with more refined stitching around the neckline so you can dress it up under a vest, cardigan sweater, or jacket. No serging stitches, embellishments, or logos should show on your best basic. They limit versatility. Midhip length allows more styling options. If made of all cotton, select a size larger to allow for shrinkage. A well-fitted pullover skims your body. If it clings or forms stress wrinkles around the bust, back, or arms it is too small.

More about pullover shirts.....

Gradually add on a short sleeve, a 3/4 length sleeve, and a long sleeve knit top for comfort all year round. A long sleeve black pullover or turtleneck is a surprisingly stylish and sophisticated layering piece for cold weather worn under shirts, sweaters, vests, tunics, and jackets. My favorite are silk turtlenecks that come in light-, medium-, and heavyweights from WinterSilks. Again, the day it looks faded, retire it to your yardwork clothes or the rag bag.

Add complementary color pullover tops to coordinate with added print shirts and pants. Sleeveless tank tops are comfortably cool under your blazer in hot, humid weather. A black tank layers for business as well as elegant evening occasions. A savvy, narrow striped top is so slimming under your blazer.

You'll be ready for a night on the town, cocktail or company party when you add a single shiny or sparkly top in lame', charmuse, or metallic knit that will give you years of wear. Choose your dressy knit top in your eye or blush color or one of those jewel tones I listed earlier. Make your entrance wearing your blazer, removing it when you want to look and feel more relaxed and approachable. While sleeveless or spaghetti straps may appear dressier, wear them only if your arms and chest are smooth and firm. Again, if the top is sleeveless, make sure the armholes are high enough so your bra is not exposed. Other options include a beautiful, softly draped neckline and/or sleeves, adding elegance to your look.

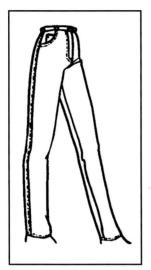

5-Pocket Jeans
Slightly Tapered

Dress Jeans

These jeans are intentionally more refined, dressier, dress-jeans for a nicer day or night out. Wear them with a cotton tee, broadcloth, silk or satin sportshirt, and black blazer or black leather jacket. The perfect pair of dress-jeans are worth the time it takes to find. By "perfect pair" I mean clean jeans, without fading, fraying, or whiskering, and of course in a flattering style sized to fit. Ignore the numbers and go for the look.

Something most people don't know is that faded, stained, whiskered, cut, frayed, or ragged jeans date you, brand you as defiant, rebellious, or generally unwilling to take direction. They attract attention to the contrast in line and color, whiskers to the crotch. Do you really want all viewer attention down there?

You're looking for a pair of jeans that accommodates your body perfectly, not exposing or emphasizing any body area that's proportionally large—a belly, bottom, or side-thigh bulge. A little stretch in the fabric of your jeans allows a little "give" over your bottom and thighs—no more than two percent stretch fiber.

Style options to try include straight leg, bootcut, slightly tapered, or slightly flared, but bootcut is generally most flattering and versatile. They look terrific with sandals, sneakers, flats, heels, shoe boots, or boots, and are classic so won't go out of style. Also classic is a natural waistline. High-rise jeans lengthen the look of your legs, low-rise lengthen the look of your torso but shorten your legs—not smart unless you've got long legs. Like them or not, these days jeans go almost everywhere. Choose dark wash blue denim for a more sassy, slimming, and sophisticated look—even relatively elegant looking black jeans if you like. The hem should fall at the heel of your shoe, about 1/8th to 1/4th inch off the floor.

More about jeans.....

Some higher quality dressy denim is referred to as "Premium," "Ringspun," or "Japanese" denim. More refined in the manufacturing process, they are higher priced. Wash them with extra care, turning them inside out. Dry on delicate or snap them into shape and hang to dry. Press lightly.

Choose a lighter blue wash for an everyday, outdoorsy look and white for fresh-looking spring and summer wear. I build for clients, whole denim clusters for at-home and community wear. I include a variety of tops—pullover tank, tee, and turtleneck or mock turtleneck depending on neck length; button front shirts to wear on their own or layer as a shirt-jac over a tee. Additional style options for knit pullover tops include jewel or crew neck, scoop or V-neck, band or collared; short, three-quarter, and long sleeve lengths. I often include a denim vest and/or jacket. You have options depending on the weather and your personal style. Denim tends to be a muted wardrobe neutral in color, allowing you to coordinate it with just about any color top you like. The exception might be a greenish-blue that fights with the blue denim. The best patterned tops play off the tiny white striations created by the denim weave—a tiny, tiny stripe or a mottled splotchiness in the pattern itself.

If you're set on skinny jeans, be careful. They tend to be unflattering on many bodies. Be sure to allow enough ease through the hip/thigh and crotch area to be more flattering and comfortable. That said, skinny jeans do not belong on any body with a belly, big bottom, or side thigh bulge! Trouser style jeans with flat-lying front pleats can be the most flattering on most figures. To balance your bottom, a slightly flared pant leg can do the job. Straight-leg styles may be cuffed. Choose a pair without pockets to eliminate any bulk. Consider jeggings as you would leggings, intended to be worn with tunic length tops.

More about low-riders? Mid-rise? High rise? Natural waistline? These are the questions I get due to confusion about where to wear your pants, especially jeans. I could talk all day. People have not a clue where their own waistline is anymore. Retail clerks and fashion reporters don't know either. With my client's permission, I reach out, centering my hands at her narrowest width, generally between the base of the ribs and the top of the hip bone. Instant panic. "No-o-o-o," they may wail. "My waist is way down here," has been their war cry as they are used to cinching their belt so tight they've forced a second indentation into their mid-torso, with the tell-tale "muffin-top" lopping over their belt. The low-rider pant is not necessarily more flattering to the tummy or the hips. If you've got a short upper torso and long legs, it's an option to used with care. Otherwise, low riders visually lengthen the look of the upper torso and shorten the look of the legs—exactly what you don't want for a slim-line look. Take your time to find the brand and cut that fits you best. Again if needed, get the jeans altered, tailored to fit your waist. This is accomplished by taking in the necessary width in the center back seam at the waist and tapering into the original seam at about the full hip-level. It works.

An alternative to jeans are sporty chinos or khakis as they're often called. Moderately priced, comfortable when well fitted, and versatile, chinos can easily become your relaxed weekend wear. Basic in style, you can dress them up with your white shirt and cardigan, vest, or jacket, then down with a knit tee. Wear them with loafers or short shoe boots. Finish your outfit with a stone or shell pendant strung on a leather cord, or try a sporty side-tied scarf.

Trench Coat

Trench Coat

How many times have you seen someone, in an effort to stay warm, wearing a plaid or tweed coat that looks like a holdover from high school? It happens. To solve that wardrobe problem you need to acquire an iconic trench coat, a classy classic, a necessary staple because it never goes out of style and is available at all price levels. It's a timeless piece that you can wear with everything from your favorite jeans with boots to a little black dress with heels. Select a single or double breasted style with collar and lapel—single if you want to wear it open. A trench coat works for every occasion if it's longer—hemmed just below your calf so skirts and dresses don't show below. It's also warmer than a short one.

Khaki tan is the classic color for a trench coat, but black is an option that doesn't show the soil, looking rather elegant for evening. Styled with epaulets—shoulder tabs—the look is more sportive, but even that gets dressed up when it's ivory colored or made of fabric with a little sheen for evening. Self-belted, it shapes your waist for a flattering fit. You want a trench coat to fit your shoulders just a little loose so you can layer it over sweaters and jackets when it's cold. Sleeves shouldn't bind when you reach. I love a trench coat designed with a capelet, the extra layer of fabric that sits over the chest and upper back to ward off the rain.

More about trench coats…..

The perfect spring and fall transitional piece, you can pick a trench coat that comes with a zip in-and-out lining. It's a stylish yet practical option for year-round wear and for travel. You can opt for a midthigh length trench if you plan to wear it only with pants or jeans. Nix any embellishment or decorative pockets that detract from the classic sophistication. If it's you, opt for a second coat just for fun, make the surprise element be the color. I've found quality trench coats in red, royal blue, burgundy, teal blue-green, and dark brown to coordinate with a particular cluster of clothes. Wear a trench fully buttoned and belted or let it hang open for a totally relaxed look. You can always dress up the look of a trench coat with a large, richly patterned scarf, rauna, or pashmina draped or looped around your shoulders.

When living in a very cold climate and often out of the car, you need a basic classic winter coat, generally out of wool to be warm enough. It, too, comes in trench style'or similar. I highly recommend a black, double-breasted, belted wrap coat with collar, lapels, and raglan sleeves. It adjusts to cover your neck, fits over whatever you've layered underneath, and doesn't show soil and longterm wear. Why dress in your best clothes, spend time and money on your hair and makeup, then finish with amazing jewelry, only to top it all off with a coat that looks like you found it at a flea market? Don't. Make your total look special, fantastic! Seen first, it makes a powerful, polished impression, first and lasting.

Top Ten Clothing Essentials

Semi-fitted
Tailored Suit

Princess-seam Suit

Softly-tailored Suit

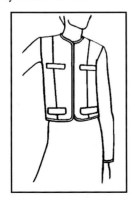

Untailored Chanel Suit

That's it

The top ten clothing essentials for virtually every wardrobe. The best thing about having your closet stocked with these basic, classic wardrobe pieces is that it's very hard to go wrong with whatever you put together. You can feel generally safe in your styling combinations with these pieces. But a few frequently asked questions remain to be answered.

What About A Matched Suit?

Looking back on this list you see that the first three items—jacket, skirt, and pants—selected in the same fabric and color constitutes a matched "suit." Together they provide you with endless variety in mixing pieces. Yes, a matched suit of clothes. Many Generation X and Y women have fallen victim to the now cliché, "Oh-h-h matchy, matchy, matchy," said with a condescending sneer. Why? It's intended as a put-down to the matched suits their mothers and grandmothers wore. Why? In the effort to establish their independence from parents, fashion writers of the age latched onto the matched suit as though there's something wrong with it, something to be avoided, something not to be caught dead in. Nonsense! Get over it. Don't let anyone limit your options like that. What's amusing, trying to get out of the hole they dug for themselves, fashion writers next started talking in terms of "sets." Call it a set or a suit, it's a matching top and bottom, with the pieces totally unlimited as to exactly what they may be. Don't let yourself get sidetracked by someone trying to control the fashion trends and how you use your clothing dollars. A matched suit gives you the option of instant harmony and more in the way of mixability, versatility, and economy. Some suit retailers offer two, even three styles in their jackets, skirts, and slacks. Some offer a matching shirt and knit shell or cardigan. They are marvelous options for selecting the best style for your body and your psyche. I buy multiple suit pieces for myself and my clients. To really get your money's worth, it makes sense to wear these essential pieces as a matched suit and as separates with other pieces in your closet. Enjoy your freedom to choose. Let yourself have fun with fashion.

What About Black?

Yes, many fashion writers and bloggers advise a black blazer, black pencil skirt, black pants, black, black, and more black. It makes sense. Black works with virtually anything, anywhere and doesn't show the little bits of soil accumulated in the wearing. Black communicates visual authority, boosting credibility. It allows you to feel more in charge of yourself and the situation. But next we read from some of the same fashion writers and bloggers, "No more black," "Don't wear black," "Get rid of all black," and the idea is passed around without thinking, from one blogger to another until it's become the trend. Ridiculous! There's no logic and it's limiting your choices again. Black is a fantastic wardrobe neutral, looking modern, mixing well with every other color, is relatively slimming, and looks clean longer. Black is a fail-safe option for business and evening occasions, but it also works with daytime denim and a myriad of tops for busy moms on the run. Wear black in combination with one of your personal body colors and you're beautifully part of the color scheme with your clothes. You're not, however, stuck with or without black. Remember that rich, dark wardrobe neutrals such as charcoal, gray, navy blue, brown, olive green, forest green, teal blue-green, plum, burgundy, and cinnamon rust are wardrobe neutrals and can be used in place of black. Pick what you love and is available when you need it. ……………………………………………………..Red can actually pass the test, coordinating well with all the wardrobe neutrals. I have a cluster with core pieces in red and a variety of classy, sassy red shoes. I have clients who love working with red and camel, red and charcoal, red and black, and the list goes on.

What About Sexy?

The whole world is hung up on the idea of virtually everything having to be "sexy,"—sexy clothes, sexy car, sexy toothpaste, sexy you name it! So what does sexy really mean? I asked that question to a very diverse focus group of college students. The bottom line, it came down to, "Sexy means I want you to look at me and think about having sex with me." It's really a matter of casual sex—any one, any time, any place—which leads to unwanted diseases, pregnancies, abortion, and abuse. Do you really want to go that route? On another occasion, I was dressed for business travel and an airport clerk looked at me exclaiming, "Oh, you look so sexy!" Seizing the moment, I invited her to tell me more of what she meant by that. "Oh, you look so puttogether, so pretty." Following up on this, I have discovered that many young people just toss the word "sexy" around, being very naïve about its real meaning. Blatant sexual appearances seldom lead to anything worth having. We can all do without "too much information" which we are often exposed to. Trying to look sexy-alluring 24/7 leads to trouble and interferes with the achievement of your worthy life goals. Instead of the word "sexy," try using the word "romantic." Subtle romantic cues in clothing color, fabric drape, style shape, and jewelry do wonders to make you memorable. Mindful dressing that leads to positive first and lasting impressions will serve you well.

Surplice Dress

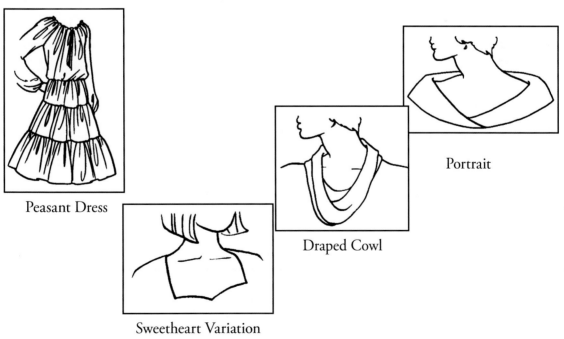

Peasant Dress

Sweetheart Variation

Draped Cowl

Portrait

More Tailored

Less Tailored

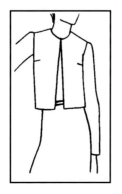

Softly Tailored

Untailored

What About Formal, Tailored Styling?

By virtue of design, tailored is tubular—a tube around your torso, tubes around your arms and legs. The most tailored looking clothing styles are designed with straight lines, more angular shapes, and generally longer styling. A blazer jacket, pencil straight skirt, and slacks are tubular, tailored looking styles. They are time-tested basic classics, always in style. They are visually more authoritative, communicating more stability, credibility, capability, and productivity. The look contributes to a stronger, more powerful and purposeful impression on yourself and others.

Less tailored or softly tailored and untailored looking clothing styles are designed with curved lines, more rounded shapes, and generally shorter styling. A bolero jacket, full skirt, and capris pants are less tailored looking styles. They tend to be less classic, going in and out of style more often. They are visually more approachable, communicating flexibility, familiarity, sociability, and availability. The looks contribute to a softer, more relaxed impression on yourself and others. And no, Mary Jane strapped shoes do not work with a tailored looking suit.

Finding your personal degree of balance between tailored authoritative looks and untailored approachable looks takes some real thought—mindfulness. You will tend to have a preference toward one side or the other, contributing to your personal style. If your personal style is towards untailored-romantic, you might choose a jacket with a softly draped cascade collar. If it's toward tailored-sportive, maybe you'll choose a safari style jacket or vest. If it's towards extremely tailored-dramatic, suppose you choose a leather jacket with a diagonal zip-front closure. The options have always been out there to express your personal style.

But you'd better get buying the looks you'd really like to have, 'cause they're gonna be gone. Most American women aren't wearing tailored or even softly tailored looking clothes anymore. Dressing in totally casual, untailored, generally ill-fitting jeans and t-shirts, we are losing the companies that used to carry nicer clothing in tailored and softly tailored styles. They're going out of business and the list of those already gone is long. So predictable. So sad for the economy and for us—our loss of beauty and civility!

I could write about jeans and the casual dress downtrend for pages and pages. As a matter of fact, I already did. In 1985 I wrote "America's Going Down the Tube in a T-Shirt." In 1995 Newsweek

More Tailored

Untailored

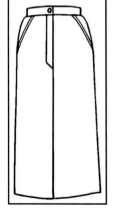

More Tailored Skirt

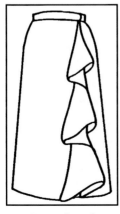

Untailored

declared America a "Nation of Slobs" in casual dress. Have you ever looked up the word "casual?" Depending on the dictionary, the word "casual" means "without thought, careless." The phrase "business casual" is an oxymoron, the words contradicting themselves.

Whatever the business, to succeed we cannot afford to be thoughtless, careless. Self presentation in the workplace can have significant consequences regarding your assignments, your influence, your income, and ultimately your success. So dress like you mean business no matter where you work. It's a matter of image from the outside in. Dressed in a top with a collar, for example, you'll feel more capable, stand taller, and speak more clearly. No, jeans are not neutral. No, they don't really go with everything and everywhere. But assuming we think so, we lapse into an utter lack of conscious thought—and it's said that giving no thought, never ends well.

Both men and women tell me, "I didn't get the job, the promotion."

I say, "Get out of your jeans and t-shirt."

They say, "My kids don't listen to me, don't do what I teach them, don't behave."

I say, "Get out of your jeans and t-shirt."

They say, "My husband doesn't look at me like he used to, doesn't hold me close."

I say, "Get out of your jeans and t-shirt."

They say, "I'm bored with my life—getting depressed." I say, "Get out of your jeans and t-shirt.

They say, "But Judith, if I buy that [piece of clothing], I'd have to have someplace to go."

I say, "That's the idea. Go someplace! Get involved! Get a life!"

End point: I'm talking about you getting more effectively involved in the home, school, church, community, and/or in the workplace— wherever it works for you. A more tailored looking appearance, to the degree that works for you, goes a long way toward looking better, thinking, feeling, and acting better. People treat you better. Life gets better. It works!

Top Ten Accessory Essentials

Complete your outfits with essential accessories. Accessories can meet many needs—physical, psychological, social, and aesthetic needs. They can help balance your body build, repeat some of your personal coloring and/or add needed contrast, update your look, lead attention throughout your outfit to one dominant point of interest or emphasis, and communicate something about your values, interests, personality, roles, and goals.

Flat Shoes

Flats can be as comfortable as they are chic! Flats are always an option, often a must, depending on where you're going. The variety of styles available is never-ending. Simple ballet flats and similar styles pair with just about anything, come in all prices, and are year-round options. Those with rubber soles are easy on your feet but more polished than sneakers. Being good for your feet doesn't have to mean boring. A deep U-shaped or V-shaped vamp is so slimming to your legs. You could also consider a narrow ankle strap.

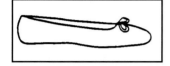

Unstructured Ballet Flats

Black is basic to go with your essential clothing pieces in black, but if you've chosen another wardrobe neutral color, follow through with the same color in your flats. Options include charcoal, navy, brown, olive, forest, teal, plum, burgundy, and rust to go with core clothing pieces—no nude unless they match or blend with the outfit. Avoid attention-getting embellishment, such as bows, and buckles, and no Mary Janes strapped over your instep—often bulky and childlike.

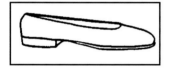

Structured Ballet Flats
or Slip-on Skimmer

Another good option is an inch thick wedge which tends to provide its own cushion. Wear flats or wedge-shaped shoes with tailored trousers, straight pencil skirts, or floral sundresses in everything from gingham to denim, suede or suedecloth, and even velvet. If you're wearing heels by day, I recommend that you carry a pair of flats in a tote or brief-bag, ready for a change of pace.

More about flats.....

Add-ons, after you've got your basics, might include leopard print flats to spice up your look. Sandals for summer can also come later. Leather loafers, canvas sneakers or running shoes could be on your list for exploring a new city, working out at the gym, or hiking in the hills.

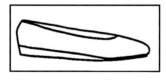

Narrow Wedge

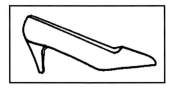

Pump

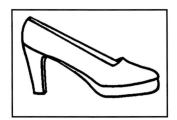

Platform Pump

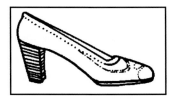

Sport Pump

High Heel Shoes

Black leather, patent, or suede pumps are reliable, classic basics that can take you from class to cocktails, boardroom to ballroom, and yes, from festival to funeral. Designed with a closed toe and heel, pumps have withstood the test of time because they don't attract attention down to your feet. For comfort and long wearlife, opt for an almond shaped toe, not pointy toes. Pumps are available with 1, 2, and 3-inch high heels that come in a variety of widths, from slim and shapely to solid stacked leather walking heels. Pass on short kitten heels that look more like you squashed the heel. Pass on stiletto high heels until you acquire a more wearable pair of heels. You really need to be able to wear your pumps for 5 to 8 hours. Fit for comfort and don't expect to "break them in." You can't conquer the world if your feet hurt. Again, be smart and carry your flats in your tote or brief-bag for a quickchange when needed. Opt for a slimming V-shaped vamp if you can find them. Avoid bulky, frumpy looking pumps. You want streamlined styles. If you've got to move from day to evening without changing your clothes, wear your white shirt, black pencil straight skirt, and awesome black heels!

More about heels…..

If you're building your basics around a wardrobe neutral color other than black, such as wardrobe neutrals in charcoal, navy, brown, olive, forest, teal, plum, burgundy, and rust, then buy your heels to match—no nude unless they match, blend, or coordinate with your clothes. Why no nude? Unless your clothes are also nude or nearly so, they provide no base for your outfit—there's no visual connection to the floor. And let's stop pretending. Nude heels don't really elongate the look of your leg. The look is like you forgot to put on some shoes. Truth is, it's higher heels that make your legs look longer, leaner. To keep pumps basic, a minimal peep-toe will pass, but avoid embellishment, bows, and buckles, and still no high heel Mary Janes.

Eventual add-ons may include a pair of red shoes to introduce that pop of color and make you feel a bit sassy, then gold or silver strappy heels to take you dancing—so much fun to wear.

Brief Bag

Tote Bag

Invest in a quality black leather, basic, classic, rectangular structured, tote bag so you carry your things with style. Got all that? It's part of your outfit and total impression. Choose leather or an excellent imitation leather. Suede is less durable than leather. No pouch style bag for things to get lost and banged around in. No clutch or handle style bag to pre-occupy your hands. Make sure you love this essential bag because it's meant to be an everyday bag for everything you need for everywhere you go. Medium to large is the size to look for, the size in proportion with your body size. A huge bag easily overpowers a petite figure. You need two or three separated sections and pockets inside the bag, with a shoulder strap to free your hands—a secure cross-body bag if needed.

Shoulder Strap Tote

Shop for a zippered closure to keep sneaky hands out. It's nice when you find a quality bag that has metal feet on the bottom so you can set your bag down without it getting dirty or falling over. Wardrobe neutral colors offer you other options as with your shoes but should coordinate well with all your wardrobe essentials. Avoid embellishment as it limits versatility. Avoid buckles all over the bag because they take too much time to open or close. No designer name or initials on your bag. Daily essentials you might carry in your bag include your portfolio, laptop, or tablet, another top and/or shoes for evening, a book, a snack, whatever. Clean out your bag, polish, and repair regularly.

If you want to switch handbags to go with a particular outfit, don't assume you have to spend a small fortune. Watch the sales for quality leather bags or the most authentic looking faux leather bag you can find. Seasonal textured fabric or straw, colored, or patterned bags are fun to have. Light or bright colors are acceptable for creative or casual business bags, although lighter colors show the soil and scratch marks more readily than darker colors. Choose them large enough to hold your small black basic clutch bag and you're off without a fuss.

Clutch Bag with
Detachable Chain

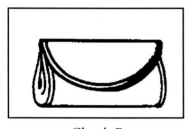

Clutch Bag

Clutch Bag

A small black leather clutch bag can hold your most needed items including ID, keys, cards and cash, cell phone, medication, reading glasses, and lipstick or lip gloss. Notepad, pen, and tissue belong in a section of the tote. Carry this basic clutch bag inside your tote or brief bag. Come evening take out the clutch, pull out the shoulder chain strap and be off, still hands free. In black, it doesn't readily show the with soil or body oils transferred by your hands. Don't stuff your clutch bag. It shows.

After you have these basic bags, you might want to be prepared with a more elegant evening bag. Add on a clutch in fabric or leather, shiny or beaded in black, cobalt, gold, or silver. The options are endless.

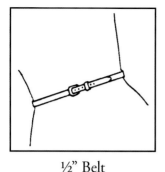

½" Belt

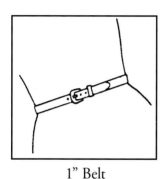

1" Belt

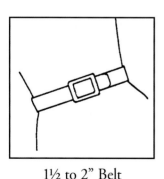

1½ to 2" Belt

Belt

A belt is essential if you need it to hold up your skirt or your pants, but this isn't usually its purpose. A belt serves to complete or finish the look of an outfit, often working as a focal point at the waist. The bigger the buckle the greater the attention it gets. If you wear a large belt buckle, then all other accessories should be less noticeable or subordinate to the belt buckle. If you don't have a natural waistline indentation, wear a belt over a top, tunic, or dress bloused at the waist. In this way a belt can create the look of a waistline indentation for a more feminine shape. Worn under a jacket, sweater, or vest, the visible buckle draws attention inward to itself, also creating the illusion of a slimmer waist. It may serve to hold a top in place and camouflage a pop tummy.

A basic black leather belt is a skinny ½-inch or 1-inch wide. I use both regularly. The most basic belt is black with a black leather buckle. Choose belts that have metal buckles in gold or silver so it matches with the metal in your jewelry.

More about belts.....

A 3-inch belt makes a real statement, and yes, most women can wear one. If you've got a pop tummy, let the buckle fill in the indentation between the midriff bulge and pop tummy for a smoother silhouette. Or, wear a marvelous belt positioned on your high hip curve and let it drop a little in front to sit smack on your belly bump. I know what you're thinking, but it really works. My clients love learning this technique. Blouse your top at the waist, then the buckle below gives the viewer something to look at instead of the belly. Layer your blazer, vest, or shirt-jac over all, recessing your body and slimming your entire appearance.

If you have a noticeable midriff bulge, wide waist, and a muffin top, do not wear tight fitting clothes or a belt that draws more attention to whole area. Generally, do not cinch a belt just below your bust, empire style. The body is generally thicker there than at the waist and a belt emphasizes the thickness for a bulky appearance. And never belt over a big, bulky sweater or you'll just look thicker and bulkier yourself.

When you're ready or when you see a marvelous belt in a coordinating color or fabulous texture in your price range, consider adding on. The finished look can be exactly what you need to change the look of the clothes from day to evening and/or from drab to fab. A satin cord or braid adds textural contrast for evening. Seasonal add-ons might include a rope belt with an arrangement of wooden beads or shells at center-front. Both offer terrific textural interest to a basic outfit.

Jewelry

Some outfits look boring or unfinished without some jewelry. You may first think of fine metals and precious gemstones, but not all lifestyles, personal styles, or budgets allow this. Happily, there are many casual to dressy options available to you. It's smart to wear or take shopping with you the clothes you want to accessorize. Start with relatively simple basic, classic pieces that work with virtually everything. You can progress to what we call "statement pieces" if you like, something bolder that can't be missed and resonates with you. Look for jewelry that signals your commitment to quality—nothing cheap looking or cliché. Pieces include:

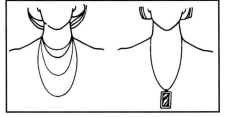

Layered Chain Necklace

Pendant Necklace

Necklace: You can begin with a set of gold or silver chains to layer as you like. Mixed metals are another option, available in many weights. There are many sources in a mall, often at a kiosk and definitely in department stores at reasonable prices. While you're there, get a polishing cloth to keep your smooth metal jewelry looking clean and shiny. Diamonds may be "a girl's best friend" but rhinestones or cubic zirconia work just about as well—without the worry in case of loss or theft. A strand of cultured pearls is lovely for a classic or romantic look and comes in several lengths, including multiple strands or ropes. No, you don't wear pearls with a polo shirt. I like to see a mix of metal and pearls. My personal style is a remarkable pendant hanging from a long chain or cord. What's yours going to be?

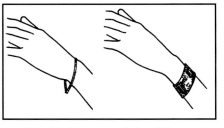

Single-chain Bracelet

Metal Expansion Bracelet

Bracelet: A gold or silver chain bracelet is a great beginning piece of basic jewelry, pearls if you prefer. If you wear both gold and silver metals, choose a bracelet that combines both metals—pulling together your other gold and silver pieces. Bigger statement bracelets come later, after you define or refine your personal style.

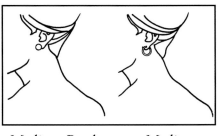

Medium Bead Earring

Medium Loop Earring

Earrings: Dress up and finish any outfit with metal or colored earrings that catch the light and brighten your look. You can't go wrong with earrings in matching gold, silver, or mixed metals in a stud, bead, or loop style. Loops can get a bit too big for business but are great for evening. For that reason it's nice to have a few different sizes for day and evening—nickel, quarter, or half-dollar sizes in 1/16- to 1/8- to 1/4-inch widths. Other options include pearl and diamond or diamond-looking studs. If metal shows, match it with other metals in your jewelry. Colored earrings are a way to bring clothing color up to your face, making you part of the color scheme with your clothes. The repetition of color creates instant harmony.

Ring: Gold, silver, and pearl rings are plentiful in a myriad of styles for you to choose from. I have gold and silver signature rings I rotate depending on my outfit. They're pounded metal about 5/8-inch wide, and worn on my pinky finger. If you have vintage pieces handed down in your family, by all means wear them. If you choose to wear more than one ring at a time, their sizes must progress from extra-small, to small, to medium, to large, and so on progressively. To appear harmonious, one ring must be dominant and all others subordinate or less important.

Watch: Choose a slim watch with a simple leather band, with gold or silver trim—so much classier than telling time from your cell phone. Dress it up with a slim chain bracelet in a matching metal. Again, a watch made of mixed metals is an ideal choice, pulling together whatever metals you want to wear in other jewelry. A big sports watch is not a basic and tends to be too sportive, never able to be dressed up.

A piece of legacy jewelry is something passed down through generations—your mother's pearls, grandmother's brooch, or greatgrandfather's watch or tie pin. A statement piece or not, it has great sentimental value that makes you stand a little taller and shine a little brighter. After you've got the basics and maybe a piece of legacy jewelry, add on carefully, the costume jewelry you want to go with particular outfits.

Glasses

Glasses are essential for those who need them to see where they're going and what they're doing. If that includes you, a basic, classic, attractive pair of glasses that works with all or most of your clothes and other accessories is essential. Basic doesn't mean boring. It means simple in style, neutral in color, and without ornamentation so they go well with your entire wardrobe and are appropriate for the many occasions in your life.

Attention to detail is important, particularly on or around your face. Glasses never looked so good. Glasses with dark frames add darklight contrast needed by fair haired women who want to wear black clothes. Rimless, beveled glasses work well with all clothing colors, best on women with darker hair. Gold or silver frames, or both make sense, depending on the metals you choose in your jewelry. I'd love a perfect pair in a mix of gold and silver—very difficult to find. Real or imitation tortoise shell glasses in brown, gray-brown or gray are also recommended for basic.

Your choice of shape depends on whether you want to repeat or counter the shape of your face. Round glasses counter a square face but repeat a round face, playing up the roundness as part of one's signature style if desired. Softly rounded glasses can soften the look of an angular face or features. Rectangular glasses can add needed width to a narrow face. Softly angular frames make you appear considerably more assertive. They are recommended for women in business and are particularly effective for shorter, smaller women. These options and more are out there for you to test.

More about glasses…..

Colored plastic glasses are generally poor choices for basic. Decorated, cut-out, or designer glasses are out—not basic. Choose nothing "cutesy" if you want to be taken seriously in business or leadership situations. If you are in a more creative business, you can be somewhat more creative in your selection of eyewear. Rimless, bevelededged, or tinted lenses are appropriate options. Glasses for relaxed and sportive occasions may be selected in larger styles with heavier frames. If you wear glasses less often, you have the option of buying fun and trendy styles in brighter colors. Consider gold, silver, bronze or copper frames. Consider leather or plastic frames in brown and earth-tone hues.

Sunglasses are a must for outdoor wear winter or summer and look far more chic than squinting. Worn to protect your eyes from glare and sun damage, they're also marvelous when you don't want to wear makeup but still want to add pizzazz to your look. Dark rimmed is basic, but brightly colored frames are great fun! Nonetheless, don't go for crazy-looking sunglasses that draw negative attention and fight with the rest of your outfit, prompting confusion about who you are. Two pair of sunglasses, one tinted blue or gray and another in amber allow you to change your glasses as you change your clothes and cosmetics. Think twice about mirrored lenses. They are gaudy, garish and offend many an observer on business, social, or casual occasions. Prescription and non-prescription sunglasses are available.

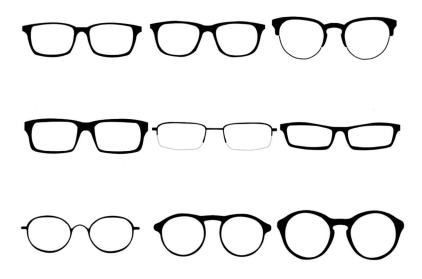

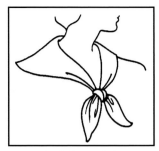

Girl Scout-Tie

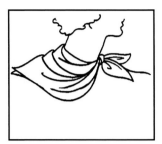

Side-Tie/
Shoulder Drape

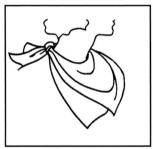

Back-Tie/Bandit

Hacking-Tie

Double-Wrap-Tie

Scarf

A scarf isn't worn just to keep your neck warm. I am always delighted by the way it adds a quick dose of personal style, visual movement, and greater interest to finish an otherwise plain looking outfit. Choose a solid color that repeats or complements your personal coloring, or pick a wonderful pattern of colors—just for fun or fancy. Pick a pattern that "pulls together" the solid colors in an outfit, looking like they belong together. Pick a pattern that includes your hair, eye, skin, or blush color, making you a part of the color scheme with your clothes for perfect harmony. Whatever the fabric, it must feel good against your skin—nothing scratchy. Working much like a collar, a scarf lifts your look and frames your face for more attention and better communication. It fills in a wide or low neckline that looks or feels a bit too bare to you. An oblong silk scarf comes first, in a pattern you feel you can wear forever. Pick three favorite ways you like to loop or knot it and enjoy.

More about scarves…..

Gradually add on some variety in scarves—square and oblong, small and large, sheer and opaque, within your budget and often on sale. If the look is really "you," wear a scarf tied around your head, around your waist, or around the strap of your handbag. Acquire a large square or oblong scarf or pashmina to wear around your shoulders as a wrap. It can be a real showstopper draped over your shoulder. I layer one over my winter coat for added warmth and elegance. Secure it with a large hat pin under a fold at your shoulder.

I keep a large black scarf in my car all winter. It's my solution to unforeseen times when I need warmth with sophistication. I love the softly dramatic touch for evening, and one size fits all. When traveling, fold a large scarf into your carry-on and pull it out when you need to ward off a chill. Once at your destination, it serves you well in a cold convention hall or conference room, for sightseeing or special nights out. A new scarf is a terrific piece to buy on a holiday or trip to bring back memories of your adventure.

While going through chemotherapy years ago, I depended on wearing my scarves as head wraps. A small square bandana became my short-hair look. A larger rectangular scarf tied with a tail became my shoulder-length hair look. I had a couple of large square scarves I tied with a very long tail for a long-hair look, topped then with a wide-brimmed hat. Yes, I had quite a variety and people noticed how great they looked. Some would say something like "Oh, so chic!" And nobody knew that underneath I was as bald as a Q-ball.

Newsboy Cap

Fedora

Picture Hat

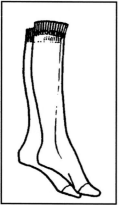

Sheer Knee-High

Opaque Tights

Hat

A hat is not something everybody thinks is essential unless they live in Alaska or Iceland, but so nice to have when you need to fix a bad hair day in a hurry! A hat is really a matter or symbol of personal style. In a wardrobe neutral color, a newsboy cap looks sporty in corduroy or wool twill. Woven or knit, a beret looks creative and romantic. A manstyle fedora adds a touch of sportive drama. You have options.

Stockings

Of course beautifully sheer nude stockings are basic—pantyhose by another name—essential in business and leadership when wearing a short skirt. If you refuse to wear stockings or the weather is hot, simply choose a longer skirt.

Consider also, two pair of black stockings for basic, one sheer and one opaque. Opt for the same in knee-high trouser socks. Opaque tights or leggings do not look dressy. They are for sporty relaxed looks and occasions only. Wear with black or darker wardrobe neutral colored clothes, not light colored clothes because they tend to look too heavy, too weighty. They work with flats, boot-shoes or booties, and boots.

While I'm writing about what you wear on your legs, leggings, jeggings, and yoga pants do not qualify as pants by any stretch of the word. The pretense only makes women look foolish. Strictly for relaxed, lounging, or actual exercise occasions, they demand a loose-fitting, thigh-length tunic top to look sharp. Quoting image professional George Brescia, "In the name of all that is decent," cover your bottom! Again, too much information!

Underwear

Not one of the wardrobe essential pieces, yet not an accessory either, quality underwear is still essential. Conselle affiliate Sarah Ward reminds us, "Before you put on anything else, foundation garments are a must!" Support yourself. A saggy, baggy body is distracting, taking attention to itself. You will be delighted by what a well-fitted bra underwear can do to enhance the fit and look of your clothes. No more round padded bras that look more like two cantaloupes stuffed up your shirt. You need a naturally molded fit with a little lift. We all need smooth-fitting seamless looking panties and slip. Yes, a slip, originated to allow your outwear to slip smoothly over your body. You really don't want to be remembered for your body bumps and bulges. If available, get yourself to a "corsetiere," a professional who knows how to give you a perfect fit.

Makeup, Makedown, Makeover

Makeup functions much like an accessory to liven you look, provide more dark-light contrast, and strengthen your visual presence.

Wardrobe Essentials

Add On Something Special

Once you have acquired all the essential clothing and accessories no closet ought to be without, you can gradually expand and diversify your wardrobe, gradually adding on greater interest via detail, color, texture, and pattern. Don't save your good clothing for some event or occasion that may never happen. And don't feel guilty about investing some money on something special. Not frivolous, indulgent, or vain, it's always a mindful matter of love plus logic before you buy. The pieces you buy must make your heart sing. When the piece adds an element of fun, function, flash, or fashion, reflects or projects your values, personality, and individuality, as well as your mood at the moment, it will become an essential part of your wardrobe. It will make you smile every time you put it on. You will enjoy wearing it. It'll make everyday a special occasion—at home, in church, school, or community, even in the workplace. At that point, the cost-per-wearing becomes worth every penny. Some women will want to add on doubles of a perfect piece, in a repeating or complementary color to their personal coloring. Anyone for triples?

Hacking Jacket

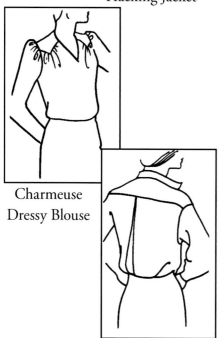

Charmeuse
Dressy Blouse

Satin Dressy Shirt

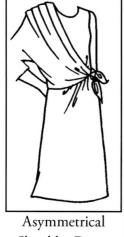

Asymmetrical
Shoulder Drape

Flare dress

Something Dressy

Instead of thinking of ways to dress down, try thinking of ways to dress up. It only takes something a little dressier to make every day or evening special. Evening occasions are just as important as daytime occasions—or vice-versa. The transition from day to evening can be fast and easy. Do it with a piece of jewelry, a scarf, shoes, or a jacket. I like to tease, saying a woman can never have too many jackets. They set the mood and can dress up the look of your wardrobe essentials immediately. Many terrific jacket styles you might consider adding are not particularly "in fashion," so they can't possibly go out of fashion— giving you longer wearlife and more individuality. More skin often says "dressy evening." Within your value system, wear a wider scoop neckline, a sleeveless or backless top. Take off the jacket and you look instantly dressier.

- Dressy jackets often become available at end-of-season sales. Fabric is the element of design that makes any jacket style look dressier—more refined, with a touch of elegance. For cold weather wear, you might choose a beautiful bouclé or velvet jacket or a tapestry blazer. Believe it or not, a black velvet blazer works over a flared blue denim dress or neat boot-cut jeans—with black boots, of course.

- Choose lace when it's hot and humid. A chiffon jacket with a cascade collar or a flared linen jacket are out of the ordinary for warm weather wear.

- It doesn't work to dress up the look of ragged jeans with an elegant evening jacket or tuxedo jacket—not even a smooth-textured business jacket. The moods they each project don't blend. The messages don't mix or match—unclear, confusing.

- You can dress up your essential dress jeans with a satin shirt, bold earrings and heels or high-heeled boots. Top off the look with a jean jacket—even a denim jacket loaded with bling.

- Soften and dress up the look of a tailored suit, in gray flannel instead of black. Wear it with a pink crepe dress shirt, silk scarf printed in gray and pink, and pearls. If pink and pearls are too feminine for you, think gray, ivory, and hunter green with gold jewelry—totally tailored.

- Back to dresses—call this one the dress of your life! It might be a stunning wrap dress in crepe fabric, fully lined to skim smoothly over your body. You might prefer a silky looking dress with a flared skirt in silk, acetate, or polyester fibers, in your best or favorite "ego" color. Powder your nose and put on some blush. Terrific!

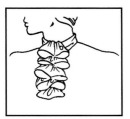

Jabot

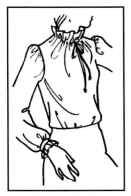

Ruffle Neck Blouse

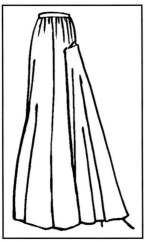

Palazzo

Rauna/Wrap

- Someone else's dress might be a bohemian inspired crinkle-cloth print in vibrant colors that just don't quit, in peasant styling with full-circle skirt that ripples as they walk.

- I've got a brown denim dress, gathered at the neck and belted at the waist—certainly not basic but great fun to wear to a picnic or the county fair.

- Some women think "ruffles" whenever they think "dressy." A ruffled blouse may be all it takes to dress up a structured classic suit—but not just any ruffle. It has to be a medium sized ruffle created with a Jabot soft fabric that lets the folds drape beautifully downward—nothing sticking stiffly out in front of you.

- A skirt instead? Consider a richly textured straight skirt in raw silk, brocade, tapestry, lace, satin, or velvet fabrics—in a solid color, stripe, animal print, paisley print, or border print. They are beyond ordinary.

- Shirts and blouses with sheen, such as charmuse, can be layered with a firmer textured fabric that works wonders to hold and smooth the body. I love to recommend a tapestry vest because both tapestry and a vest are unexpected. Suede would be another unexpected texture—perfect for a vest, mixing romantic and sportive.

- Paisley print palazzo pants worn with a simple top and sandals, ballet flats, or platform heels—fantastic! Soft-folding butterfly sleeves on the top are certainly not your everyday option but so fun and flattering.

- Slim slingback or strappy heels in black patent, matte gold, or silver metallic material go the distance. Shoes in a contrast color like red or purple, animal or floral print add pizzazz to your wardrobe essentials. Ankle straps are strikingly feminine, but be careful about where the strap hits your ankle. Lower on your ankle is more slimming. At the top of your ankle, the strap tends to make your leg look thicker.

- A dear friend went shopping for something special—the look of a lifetime she'd waited 39 years to finally buy for herself. A horsewoman herself, she bought a pair of knee-high black and brown leather tooled cowboy boots. They dress up black pants or a suede cloth dress.

- For a special dinner out or the symphony, a slim Cowboy Boots clutch bag in sparkly black, gold

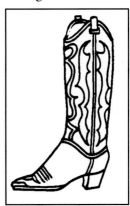

Cowboy Boots

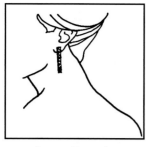

Long Dangle

Rhinestone Band

metallic, beaded, brocade, or paisley print dresses up the look—makes the occasion special. A strap is needed if you want your hands to be free.

- A piece of dressy jewelry may be a string of pearls you inherited from your grandmother, an antique gold watch hung as a necklace on a gold chain, or a magnificent ring like I bought in Florence, Italy years ago.

- While more jewelry may signal special and elegant, less can be more. Signature or vintage jewelry may be a jade ring set in gold that you bought at an antique auction. Wear it with simple hoop earrings— no fancy belt or bangles.

- A little more color, a little brighter, shouts dressier in clothes and cosmetics. It's basic brown eye shadow for business. Add colored eye shadow and/or eye liner with stronger lip color to transition from everyday to evening.

- If your hair was up, let it down to look dressier. If your hair was down, style it up to look dressier. It's amazing, but the transition from one to the other works both ways.

- No messy bun no matter how cool you think it looks. A messy bun makes you look like a follower who doesn't know how to do it, like the many who don't.

Whatever the special pieces you choose to add to your wardrobe over the years, make sure that each one makes a strong statement that is instantly recognized as being just so you and makes you feel authentic when you wear it.

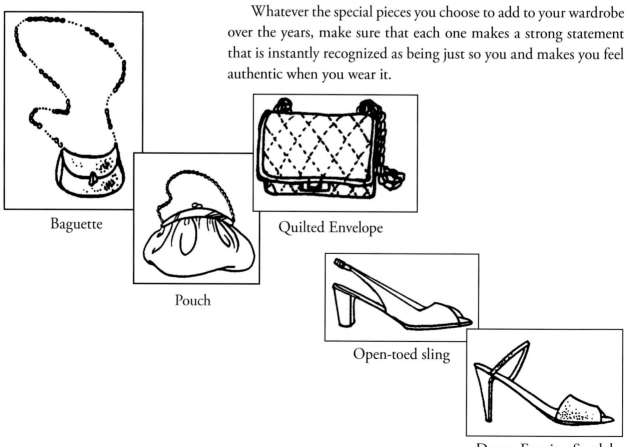

Baguette

Pouch

Quilted Envelope

Open-toed sling

Dressy Evening Sandal

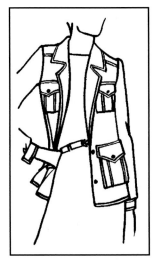

Sportive Safari Jacket

Sporty Bomber Jacket

Sporty T-shirt

Sportive Turtleneck

Something with Sporty or Sportive Styling

Both reflect an active lifestyle. Sporty styles are cute and Sportive styles are sharp—more rugged. Sporty is less tailored, designed with more curved lines and rounded shapes. Sportive is more tailored, designed with more straight lines and angular shapes. Sporty is shorter and Sportive is longer (tops, sleeves, jackets, sweaters, vests, skirts, pants, and boots). Sporty often has a smaller collar or no collar and Sportive usually has a collar including turtlenecks and jackets have a notched collar and lapels.

- Start with a black leather jacket. Yes, your core blazer can be a basic black leather jacket if it goes with all of your basic wardrobe essentials. But here I'm thinking of something more like a motorcycle jacket, aviator jacket, or bomber jacket—all quite similar. Here we go—Sporty is shorter to the waist or high hip area. Sportive is longer to the low hip or crotch level. Longer is harder to find in these styles.

- Yes, real leather will require a splurge, but real leather jackets only get better with time and wear, and they never go out of style. You might play with the style before investing by getting a low-price pleather jacket in contemporary styling at a discount fast-fashion shop like Forever 21 or H&M. They're a lot of fun for a lot of us and they don't break the bank.

- The young or young-at-heart might toughen up the look of a flirty, feminine dress with a black leather jacket. Big city girls might throw a black leather jacket over a little black cocktail dress. We can all wear black leather over a white V-neck t-shirt or blue chambray sport shirt with a great pair of well-fitted jeans, blue or black. You've got options.

- Black boots with heels look dynamite worn over leggings, yet exciting under gauchos, a skirt, or sassy dress, and assertive over jeans. Go for the almond shaped toebox, not pointy nor overly rounded. A one to two inch heel will be most comfortable, and safer to walk in. Make sure they fit snuggly at the ankle and calf, and smoothly at the top—no big gap. Shoe-boots or booties are other options with pants. To qualify as a boot, they should cover your ankle when you cross your legs.

- Pay attention to the look and feel of a sporty lightweight cotton, madras plaid shirt compared to a sportive heavyweight wool, lumberjack plaid shirt.

- Notice the difference between jeans paired with a sporty striped t-shirt compared to jeans paired with a sportive

Gauchos

turtleneck shirt then layered with a tweed herringbone jacket. Both have their place.

- Try on a sporty white cotton, crew neck t-shirt with a denim skirt and sneakers, then compare to a sportive white cotton sport shirt, dark wool riding skirt or gauchos, layered with a tweed blazer and paired with leather boots. Which look is more "you?"

- Compare a puffy, sporty ski parka with a heavy sportive shearling suede jacket. A Winter sports enthusiast may need both.

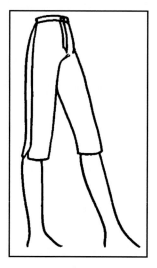

Deck Pants

V-neck Shell

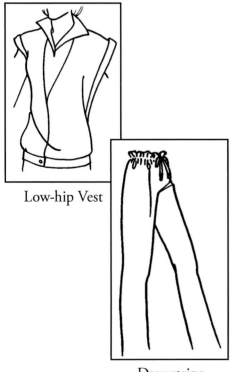

Drop-waist blouson

Low-hip Vest

Drawstring

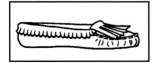

Moccasin

Something Relaxed

After business hours and on the weekend, when you're off the clock, you may want to wear something even more relaxed. I get that. I do that too. But you don't have to dress down to the level of sloppy—to looking and acting like a slob. Self-presentation and public perception never take time off—not even on the weekend. You still need to manage what you reflect or project to yourself and others. That doesn't mean you can't relax the way you look, feel, and act—to a degree. Relaxed is a good word to substitute for casual. It's more descriptive. Relaxed doesn't mean uncomfortable, unattractive, or inappropriate. Relaxed or weekend clothing is really no different than clothing that works for weekday school and community occasions. [Levels 1,2,3 on the Style Scale®]

In the movies, the moment a man wants to relax we see him loosen his tie and roll up his shirtsleeves. It's a good way to dress down, quick and easy, giving him good return on his clothing investment as he wears them into the evening. Since the 1980s we women have been rolling up our sleeves too—on shirts and jackets. It works.

From there, what can you count on to look and feel more relaxed yet nice?

- Knits, with v-necklines for more visual authority
- Chinos, khakis, or soft corduroy pants
- More colors in solids and in patterns
- Somewhat looser styling and/or fit. Never tight or binding. There's plenty of ease to sit or move as you like.
- Shorter sleeves
- Drawstring pants or skirts
- Elastic waist bands all around or in back only—again, never tight or binding.
- Take off the jacket, unless you're blessed with lots of body bumps or bulges. If so, you're still smart to wear lightweight layers. A loosefitting jacket, vest, or duster made of thinner, porous fabrics give you light-weight options. Think silk noil, gauze, lace, eyelet, and cutwork.

There is never anything that is uncomfortable about the clothes and the outfits that I recommend or style for my clients. Do you think I want to wear uncomfortable clothes? No way! It's the same for shoes. You can choose from stacked walking heels, comfy wedges, loafers, cute sneakers, ballet flats—and the list goes on.

For the record, "casual" dress is not easier to figure out or carry off well than business or dressy day wear. People think it is, but the #1 question I get centers on what is business casual, smart casual, chic casual, evening casual, and so on. Casual is not more creative nor more productive.

Don't feel guilty about investing some money for the clothes you wear at home. Your clothes affect you even when alone.

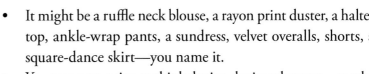

Something Fun

These periodic wardrobe additions ought to be more of what's fun for you—something that says "have fun" and enjoy the moment. Something fun can be anything you want that you have a place to wear it.

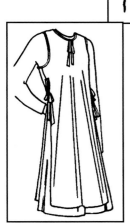

Ruffle

Overalls

Patchwork

- It might be a ruffle neck blouse, a rayon print duster, a halter top, ankle-wrap pants, a sundress, velvet overalls, shorts, a square-dance skirt—you name it.
- Yes, many are going to think denim, denim whatever—maybe a Western style denim jacket, a braided denim vest—now that's fun. I love my denim duster and it feels fun yet sharp.
- A denim dress in blue, brown, or black, particularly fun with buttons down the front so that the dress doubles worn open like a duster with pants and top beneath.
- Maybe dark wash denim jeans weren't part of your essentials, but with the essentials in your closet you now feel free to add some blue jeans just for fun—maybe with zip pockets, flap pockets, cargo pockets, embroidered pockets, drawstrings, top-stitched design details, or whatever.
- Maybe you already have the pants and now want a denim skirt. Fine. Go for it, but I highly recommend fade-free fabric and frayfree edges. Look sharp and not like a throwback from the 1990s.
- This is the time for a T-shirt with a logo or one-liner that reflects your personal style or self-branding—something you're happy to wear, and happy to share. A logo related to places you've been is popular, but never anything offensive to anyone. Colors fade and edges get stretched and rippled with wear and washing. Relegate this tee to the rag bag as soon as it looks well-worn.
- If you're a crafty lady, consider something that's been embellished with sequins, applique, embroidery, or braid. You have options.
- Do it yourself if you like. I'm talking about something that will jazz up your simple knit tops, be they tank, shell, scoop or V-neck tee, or turtleneck styles.
- Clogs, crocs, or cute, colorful, chic non-athletic sneakers are options to just hang out in. Just like upgrading your tee with a blazer or vest, these sneakers serve to change up the look of your everyday jeans or shorts. You'll have fun wearing them.

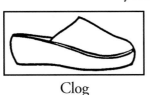

Drawstring
Gaucho

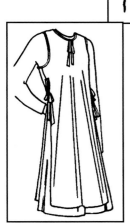

Tabard

Clog

Harache

Something Warmer

No matter where you're at, if you're cold, you're miserable. You don't want to be a pain, always complaining. Take care of yourself. Take what's needed to layer.

- A cable knit sweater, gray flannel or tweed trouser-pleat pants, a buffalo check or scotch plaid shirt, a handknit wool muffler or poncho or both, shearling lined boots, all of these function to keep you warm in cold wind, rain, sleet, or snow.
- A fleece vest layers comfortably over a cotton or silk knit turtleneck and under a straight-hanging wrap coat.
- A cashmere hoodie is more luxurious than your basic cardigan but more relaxed looking due to the hood.
- A puffy down coat takes you on errands around town, is comfortably warm, fun at the football game, and exactly what you need if you come to ski in Utah.
- Ivory wool in winter is elegant. Flannel and twill are thicker, warmer. Wear a whole outfit in ivory—ivory head to toe. It's a surprise color that is a refreshing change in the darker months.
- And of course you need a heavy winter overcoat designed with raglan sleeves to accommodate your polo or turtleneck, and blazer, sweater, or vest layered beneath. Black is basic and never goes out of style. Layer with a huge patterned scarf for a look you'll love.

Fur-trimmed hat

Crossover Sweater

Belted wrap

Sweater knit sheath

Fringed Duster

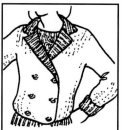

Double-breasted Sweater

Leg Warmers

Quilted Parka

Parka Variation

Something Cooler

What serves you best in the heat of summer is loosely styled clothing. You need somewhat larger necklines, armholes, sleeves, waistlines, and hemlines.

- Tank tops alone, under a shirt jac or jacket are among my favorites. A cap or short-sleeved shell ranks next.
- Three-quarter length sleeves are more comfortable than long—yet cover soft "jello" arms.
- Knee-length city shorts, culottes, cropped, or capri pants are comfortable options. Full-cut drawstring pants and palazzo pants expand your options.
- Full skirts and dresses are cooler even in heavy humidity.
- Cotton is what we think of to be cool enough in summer, but it must be lightweight cotton.
- Rayon and linen are excellent options, as are many cotton-synthetic blends. They tend to absorb body moisture which then evaporates to keep us cool.
- Thin, sheer fabrics layer nicely over a camisole.
- An airy white blouse in eyelet fabric, embroidered lace, or fabric featuring cutwork and fringe are popular.
- For years I wore a favorite painter's smock, a loose-fitting jacket made of raw silk noil. Air flow is key.
- Light colors reflect sunlight to some degree, therefore we're smart to get light-colored clothes for spring and summer.
- Switch to light blue and white jeans for summer. White denim pants and skirts look smart and chic with most warm weather tops.
- Lightweight "cool" tropical wool or viscose work well for hot-weather suiting.
- Espadrille and hurrache style shoes, and black mules are classic styles that come out every summer.
- Of course sandals of all sorts are available. For the best buys, look for your favorite styles at end-of-season sales.

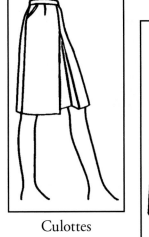

Tank

Sailor

Painters Smock

Culottes

Sarong

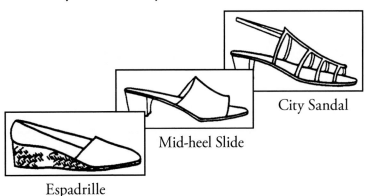

Espadrille

Mid-heel Slide

City Sandal

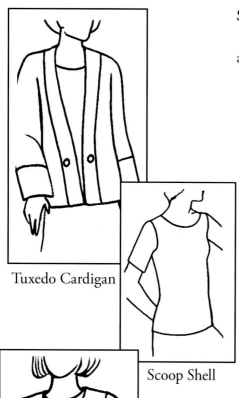

Tuxedo Cardigan

Scoop Shell

Something for Travel

In today's world, knits meet most needs, as they are lightweight and wrinkle resistant.

- Acetate-spandex, often called "slinky" is a favorite fiber for women's knitwear.
- Poly-microfiber is wonderful, but many stretch-weaves feel too heavy, stiff.
- Plan for garments that layer on and off effectively to be comfortable in heat or cold. Test before you travel.
- Your wardrobe essentials generally fit the need—as a cluster of clothes immediately ready to go.
- Jeans and a textured sweater with stone and shell necklace takes you to the beach.
- Add on a few lighter- or heavier-weight pieces depending on where you are going.
- Buy or sew a sheer rectangular print poncho for an elegant layer over a shift or sundress, capris or palazzo pants. They fold flat in your suitcase and work for dressy day or evening occasions—perfect for formal nights on a cruise.

When packing, carefully lay out your clothes flat in your suitcase, the fewer the folds the better. Fold sleeves inward from the shoulder/armhole. Fold skirts, pants, and shirts approximately in half as they lie in the suitcase. Fold jackets at the lapel breakline (where the lapel starts to roll at or above the waist). With practice, you can smoothly layer 30-garments into a medium sized suitcase, having little to no need to press when you arrive at your destination.

Asymmetrical Vest

Shirt Dress

Narrow Wedge

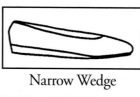

Belt Bag

Loafer

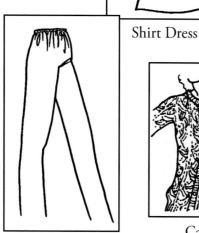

Elasticized Waist
Pull-on Pants

Cardigan

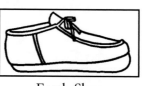

Earth Shoe

Shoulder Strap Tote

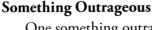

Duster Vest

Asymmetrical Hem

Surplice Maillot

Jumpsuit

Shawl

Harem Pants

Something Outrageous

One something outrageous might be exactly what lifts you out of depression or spices up your day. Call this piece of clothing an "ego item," a signature piece guaranteed to lift your spirits and get viewer attention plus a few compliments. It soon becomes recognized as looking like "You."

- Outrageous to some, red can actually pass as a sportive wardrobe neutral, coordinating well a myriad of other colors. I have a favorite winter-weight cluster with core pieces in red and a variety of classy, sassy red shoes.
- Your ego item might be a top in an unusually bold, crazy pattern of your favorite colors. Give the pattern the attention it needs by wearing it with a solid color skirt or pants.
- It might be a red, ruffle-front coat with tailored collar, worn with palazzo pants, and stilettos (only if you really know how to walk in them).
- It could be an embroidered velvet jacket you dreamed about before you went back to buy it, or a large fringed shawl.
- Maybe you could go for something out of the ordinary, like gauchos or culottes with a matching jacket or cargo-pocket vest.
- Consider the amazing jumpsuit pictured on the front of a fashion magazine.
- Picture leopard print pants, shoes, boots, or bag.
- Go ahead and buy the swimsuit that actually fits and flatters.
- Go online to find a fabulous faux fox fur coat.
- I've got a vest made out of feathers and fur—an outrageous ego item for sure.
- Save for a maxi-length sweater duster with multi-colored stripes.

Even with the top ten essentials hanging in her closet, each woman's wardrobe will still be different, depending on the design details she selects that express her personal style. Add on special pieces in the years ahead, something like those outlined previously, and you ensure creativity and individuality to the degree that you want it. Nonetheless, it's having the top ten to work with that makes the add-ons more likely to work together. Together, it's what's in your wardrobe that allows you to gain full control over the impressions you reflect or project to aid you in achieving your goals. The door to your closet is one that "…you will be more than happy to open, knowing that it holds everything you need in order to put together outfits that will have you standing tall— no matter what the day holds," agrees George Brescia, NYC image professional.

Cluster Your Clothes

Much like your collection of wardrobe essentials, a cluster is a small group of coordinated clothes put together for one particular person. While a capsule is closed-ended, a cluster is open-ended and evolves as you evolve over the years. People of all ages find this lifestyle wardrobe strategy practical, smart, and effective. Fun too!

A cost-efficient cluster includes enough garments for a variety of great looks to suit your moods and occasions. It also allows proper spacing between wearing and cleaning. It allows for gradual buying and regular replacement as needed. It ensures mix-and-matchability. You get more outfits with fewer clothes because the clothes are coordinated in style, color, fabric, and pattern—print, plaid, or stripe. A beginning cluster of five to eight pieces of clothing will do nicely for yourself and all family members.

Your wardrobe essentials function as a cluster. I started with the black as a wardrobe neutral. It's a most versatile, basic, classic core color for wardrobe essentials. I used another wardrobe neutral, white for the button front shirt. I did give you the option of a blue chambray shirt. Right there you have two different color schemes suggested. Black and white is very predictable, a traditional color scheme. Blue and black are less predictable, a little more creative. Expand your cluster by adding one new color that works with what you already have.

If you don't want to work with black, if you are essentially starting a totally new cluster, I suggest that you begin by finding a garment in a pattern (a print, plaid, or stripe) of colors you absolutely love and feel like you could wear forever. Call this your inspiration piece. Very often the garment is a top, but the pattern could be in any garment or easily a scarf.

- Ideally, within the pattern there is one or more muted wardrobe neutral colors. They go with virtually any other color. They can be worn by virtually everybody because they contain both warm and cool color used in the muting process.
- Ideally, within the pattern there is one or more of your personal body colors. Repeating your personal coloring in the clothes, you will immediately become part of the color scheme—in total harmony.
- Ideally, within the pattern there is a pleasing mix of light, medium, and dark colors that make the cluster more interesting.

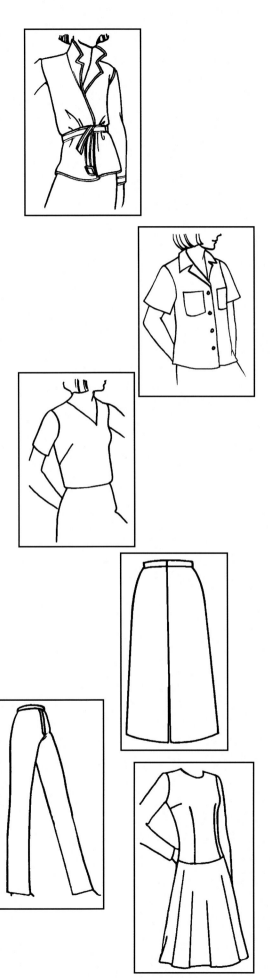

It takes about five basic pieces of clothing to work as a cluster—to mix for different looking outfits—Five Easy Pieces® as I called them in my first wardrobe videos, now classics in the field. I suggest three tops and two bottoms. No two pieces in a beginning cluster should be styled exactly alike—at least not until your wardrobe is larger. For the tops, I suggest:

- one pullover shirt,
- one button-front shirt, and
- one third-layer piece such as a jacket, sweater, vest, tunic, or duster.
- For the bottoms, I suggest: • one pant and
- one skirt.

Each piece in a cluster is distinctly different. This insures you variety in the scores of looks you can put together for different moods and occasions.

This cluster is much like your wardrobe essentials, but you can certainly choose two pants in different styles or two skirts in different styles, as needed depending on your lifestyle and the occasions the cluster is planned for. Solid colors and accessory colors come from your inspiration piece. To expand the possible outfits, add on three more pieces that include two more tops and one bottom or a dress for eight easy pieces, mixing to create from 16 to 30 or so different looking outfits. If the cluster is expanded beyond twelve pieces, feel free to include an "ego" item—something you absolutely love and can really use but doesn't necessarily go with everything else. Add on and replace clothing pieces over the years. With time you may have two, three, or five clusters—as you like and is affordable for you—phase out and create entirely new cluster as you like.

Of course, a complete wardrobe requires more than 8-12 pieces of clothing plus essential accessories. Expand your initial cluster to include limited-occasion, active sports, and essential seasonal clothing such as a coat, swimsuit, ski wear, and so on. Include necessary underwear and sleepwear. Whatever your decisions, you never need to start from "scratch" again. You can change, update or add on to what you already own as you create an efficient, workable wardrobe—one that works for you!

(To acquire more knowledge about clusters, read my book on *Cluster Your Clothes*.)

How to Arrange Your Closet

To increase the wearlife of your clothes and avoid closet clutter and confusion, hang up and put away your clothes the minute you take them off. Make this a habit. Wooden or satin padded hangers look nice but they take up too much space and you can't travel with them. On the other hand, skinny velvet-coated hangers allow no space between clothes. Rely on retail plastic hangers. The hooks conveniently swivel on the rod. Request hangers with whatever you buy, or purchase a box of shirt/dress hangers and skirt/pant hangers at a local display store. They are worth having.

Arrange your clothes on the rod in clusters, treating your wardrobe essentials as one cluster. Within each cluster, arrange the clothes from high authority to low authority—more approachable. This is the order: third-layer jacket first, then vest, then sweater, dress, skirt, pants, and finally tops—woven shirts with a collar, knit skirts with a collar, woven with no collar, knits with no collar. You can also arrange within the shirts by sleeve length—long sleeves, three/quarter sleeves, short sleeves, sleeveless, and finally spaghetti straps. Yes, you could put the jacket first, dress next, then skirt and pants—they may all be matching core pieces. Then comes the vest, sweater, and tops. You have options. The night before "tomorrow," determine what you need to wear for the next day to accomplish your goals. When you want to reflect more visual authority, reach toward the jacket side of the rod. When you want to reflect more approachability, reach toward the opposite side. Leave the hangers on the rod, marking where to return the clothes.

Make friends with the clothes in your closet. Conduct a private athome "scarecrow" party, laying out on your bed each and every outfit you can think of—top to toe. Take a quick picture of each outfit to put in a personal style file for future reference. Try on whatever you like. Get comfortable wearing them. Consider your clothes your new best friends. They present you the way you want to be seen, with your body in balance and as part of the color scheme. They should express your unique sense of self—your values, attitudes, interests, personality traits, roles, and goals. I say, "ain't clothes wonderful?!"

With these clothes waiting in your closet for you, you'll always have what you need to wear, wherever you need to go. Wardrobe essentials and cluster pieces are meant to be worn, worn out, and replaced with update versions, allowing you to stand tall as a strong leader in your home, school, church, and community, as well as in the workplace. (To acquire more knowledge about closet organization, read my book on *Closet Organization and Clothing Care*.)

Increase Your Confidence

Yes, confidence comes from having talent, knowledge, and skills. But in addition and on the most practical level, confidence comes from having the clothes in your closet you need or want for wherever you need or want to go. No matter the assignment or invitation, confidence to accept without worry comes from knowing you have something terrific to wear that's *YOU*!

Smile

While you're at it, wear a smile from ear to ear. A smile is simple, basic, and never goes out of style. It fits, no matter what your size or shape. It's free—no cost per wearing—and appreciated by all who see it. A smile is approachable and softens the look of your most authoritative outfits, yet strengthens the look of your jeans and tee. A smile has to be the most attractive thing that anyone can put on anywhere for everyone and every day. I want you to smile every time you open your closet door, seeing clothes you need and want to wear. I want you to feel joy when you get dressed, able to greet each new day with a smile, then forget about yourself and get on with what matters most—living your life to the fullest!

And remember throughout your day, "You're never fully dressed without a smile!"

Printed in the United States
By Bookmasters